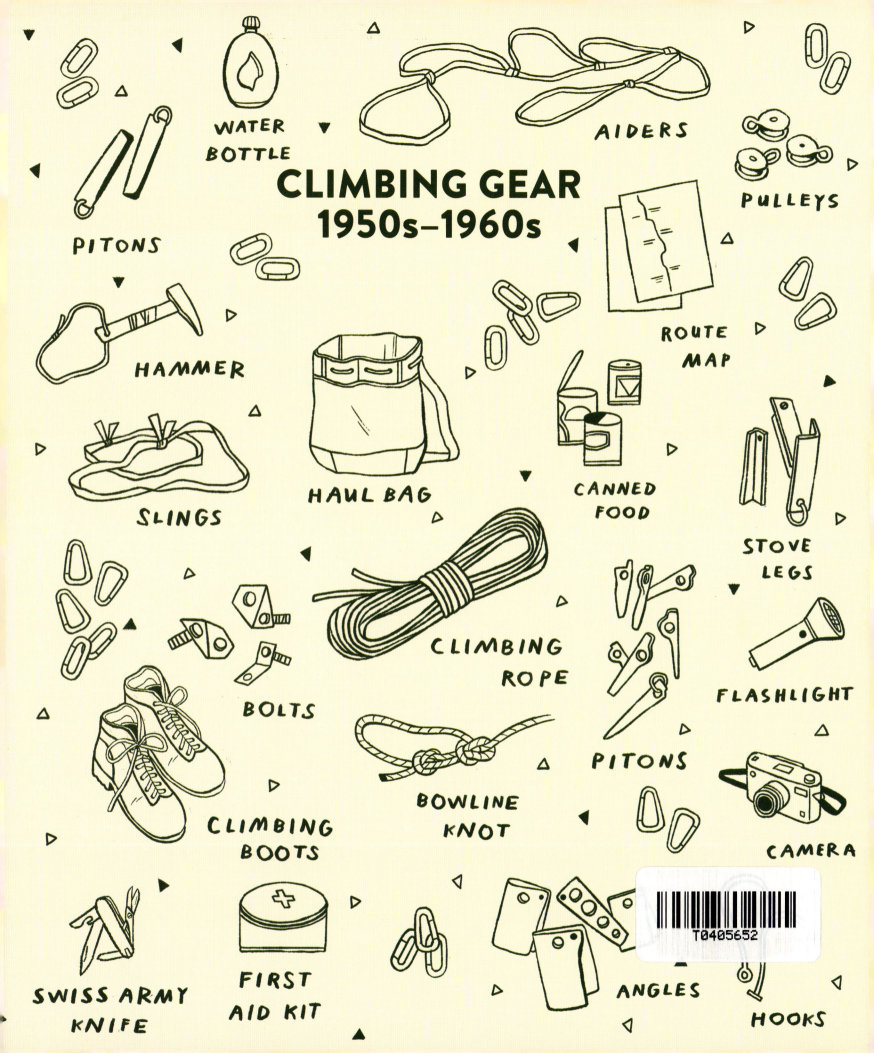

For Jake, who knows the magic of Yosemite Valley.
—K. M.

For all my climbing partners, thanks for the belay.
—S. L.

FIRST ASCENT

The Epic Yosemite Rock-Climbing Rivalry of Royal Robbins and Warren Harding

BY
KATE MESSNER

ILLUSTRATED BY
STEVIE LEWIS

YOSEMITE CONSERVANCY
YOSEMITE NATIONAL PARK

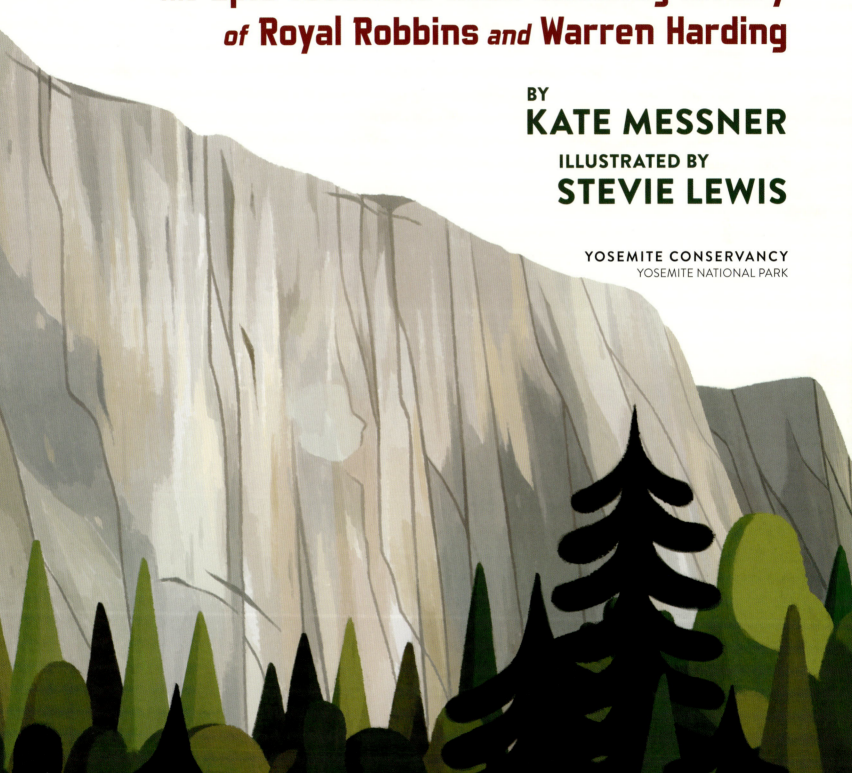

YOSEMITE
CONSERVANCY

yosemite.org

Text copyright © 2025 by Kate Messner
Illustrations copyright © 2025 by Stevie Lewis
Published in the United States by Yosemite Conservancy. All rights reserved.
No portion of this work may be reproduced or transmitted in any form without the written permission
of the publisher, except in the case of brief quotations embodied in critical articles or reviews.
Yosemite Conservancy inspires people to support projects and programs that
preserve Yosemite and enrich the visitor experience for all.
Library of Congress Cataloging-in-Publication Data is on file and available upon request.
ISBN 978-1-951179-33-5 (trade) | ISBN 978-1-951179-34-2 (ebook)
Design by Alicia Mikles
Printed in China
1 2 3 4 5 6 – 29 28 27 26 25

It might seem as if Royal Robbins and Warren Harding had nothing in common.

Royal was thoughtful and quiet. Warren was wild and loud.

Royal liked books and classical music. Warren liked parties.

But they both loved rocks.

BIG rocks.

Royal got his first taste of rock climbing in elementary school. He didn't have the happiest childhood. He wasn't great at school, and he couldn't throw a ball. But he loved scrambling over boulders on the ocean breakwall.

When Royal was about fourteen, he went climbing in the High Sierra.

It felt like magic when his hands touched that rock.

For the first time in his life, he felt *good* at something.

After that trip Royal devoured books about climbing. Soon it was all he could think about. He wanted to climb bigger rocks.

And then even BIGGER ones!

By seventeen, he was spending all his free time with climbers and tackling harder routes than anyone.

One day, an older guy named Warren Harding showed up at Tahquitz Rock.

Like Royal, Warren hadn't found much in life that he was good at. And like Royal, everything changed when his hands touched rocks. Warren had already become the first person to complete two big climbs at Yosemite National Park.

Imagine making it to the top of a difficult climb before anyone else in the whole world! That's called a first ascent, and rock climbers live for it.

It wasn't long before Royal and Warren tried a climb together—and then cooked up plans to climb something BIGGER.

In 1955, Royal and Warren set out with two friends to scale the Northwest Face of Half Dome—a two-thousand-foot ascent up a massive granite wall. No one had climbed it before.

They packed their gear and started up.

A handhold here . . .

A foothold there . . .

They climbed and climbed, but three days later they weren't even a *quarter* of the way to the top. Running low on food and water, they called off the climb and rappelled down, lowering themselves to the Yosemite Valley floor with a system of ropes.

That's when Royal and Warren realized they had one more thing in common.

They both HATED giving up.

So you might think those two climbers would make plans to return and try again.

And they did. But not together.

Two years later, Royal heard that Warren was getting ready to nab that first ascent of Half Dome with a different team of climbers.

There was NO WAY Royal was going to let that happen. He'd have to get there first.

By then, Royal knew what to expect for the first part of the climb. Before noon on the second day, he and his partners were halfway up the wall!

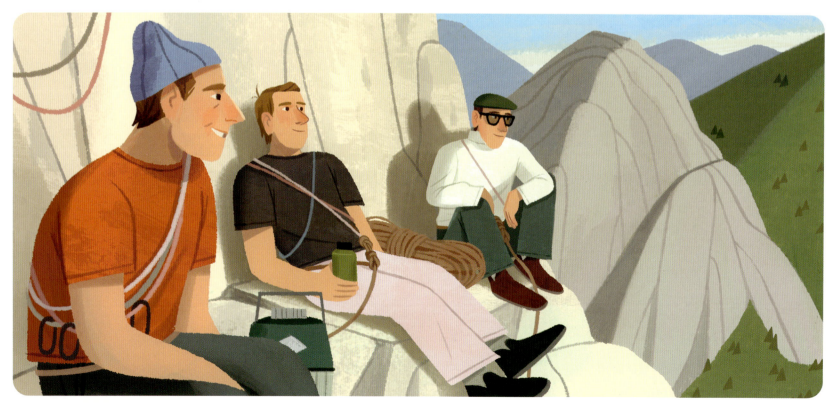

They zigged and zagged up the cliff—
a foothold here, a handhold there—
until suddenly there was nothing but smooth, blank wall.

No holds for their hands or feet.

No cracks for placing gear.

The only way to continue was to start drilling holes for bolts to climb.

It was brutal, slow work. Hour after hour in the hot June sun.

Tap . . . tap . . . tap . . .

One more bolt.

One more step up that massive face of rock.

Tap . . . tap . . . tap . . .

Finally, hanging on a rope, with no handholds or footholds in sight, Royal spotted a ledge that led to a series of chimneys, cracks so big a person could climb up inside them. If he could reach that ledge, the team would be able to keep going.

There was just one problem. Royal was nowhere near that ledge. It was *forty feet* away. So do you know what Royal did?

He had his partner lower him on the rope, and he started RUNNING across that vertical wall, SWINGING back and forth like a pendulum.

Back and forth.

Back and forth.

Thousands of feet above the Valley floor, dangling from a single metal bolt that had been placed in the rock.

Finally, Royal felt that rocky ledge under his hand

                                            and held on

                                                            for dear life.

Every night at nine o'clock, park workers pushed a cascade of embers off Glacier Point, creating a spectacle called the Firefall to entertain park visitors.

It was dazzling. It was breathtaking. And it was a perfect distraction.

That night, while all eyes were on the Firefall, the climbers switched on a flashlight.

Two flashes.

A pause.

Two more.

Their friend on the ground would understand the signal. They were okay and continuing their climb. No rescue was needed tonight.

The next morning, the climbers made their way up more narrow cracks. Above them loomed an enormous overhang and a big question: How on earth were they going to get past THAT?

Had they come all this way only to fail?

Just then, they spotted a long, narrow ledge that led around the overhang, to a final stretch of climbing. Inch by harrowing inch, they made their way across.

Thank God! (That's what they called it: the Thank God Ledge.)

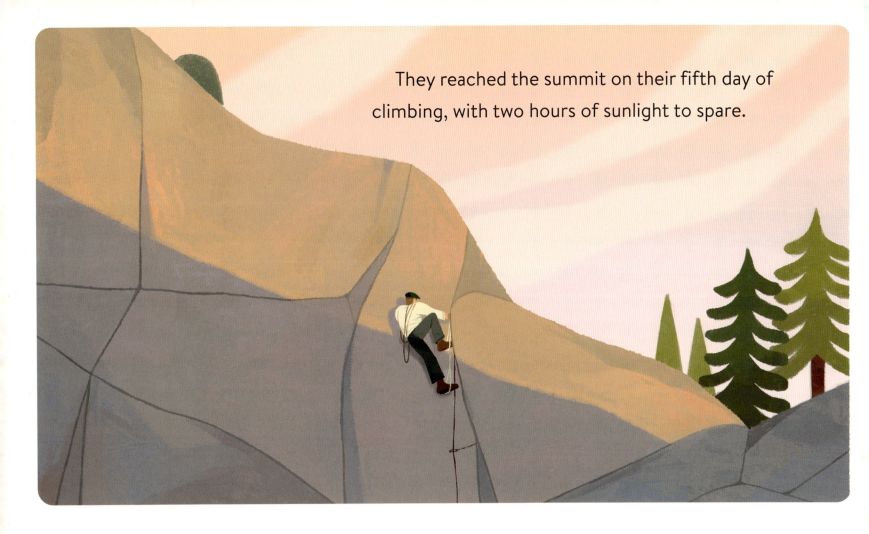

They reached the summit on their fifth day of climbing, with two hours of sunlight to spare.

And guess who was waiting for them . . .

Warren Harding!

He'd put together his own team for the climb but arrived at the base to find that Royal was already halfway to the top. So Warren didn't climb. Instead, he trekked up the eight-mile hikers' trail with water and ham sandwiches.

"Congratulations!" was what he said out loud.

But inside, he was thinking, *How am I going to top THIS?*

When Warren hiked down Half Dome, he looked up and found his answer.

El Capitan.

The granite giant of Yosemite towered three thousand feet above the Valley floor.

People said it would never be climbed.

That was it.

Warren was going to climb El Cap.

He and his partners spent hours studying the rock face, searching for a route to the top. On the Fourth of July, they started climbing.

They never planned to do it all at once. Each day, they climbed as far as they could, hauling gear to store on rock ledges. Then they fixed ropes, setting them up to climb later, and descended for the night.

Within a week, they'd pushed a thousand feet up the wall.

Tourists gathered to watch. Who were those outrageous climbers who thought they could scale El Capitan? Traffic jammed up so badly that the park rangers bellowed up at the climbers through a bullhorn.

"Get down from there!"

The team agreed to stop climbing until the busy summer season was over.

Warren returned the following spring with new partners, ready to climb.
The team pushed higher and higher.
There were wild pendulum swings.
Cracks that narrowed to nothing and disappeared.

Cracks set so wide they had to hammer in
cast iron stove legs salvaged from a dump as pitons.

There were terrifying falls...

Would their gear catch them? (It did!)

There were cold, stormy nights on ledges and exhausting days in the harness.

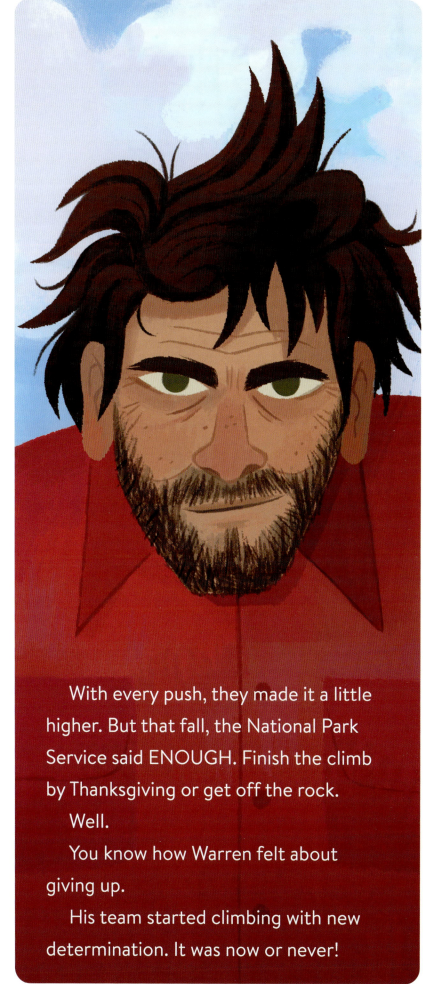

With every push, they made it a little higher. But that fall, the National Park Service said ENOUGH. Finish the climb by Thanksgiving or get off the rock.

Well.

You know how Warren felt about giving up.

His team started climbing with new determination. It was now or never!

Warren's team tried again. And again. And again. Finally, at the end of an epic twelve-day push, they climbed onto the summit of El Capitan.

Their friends were there, waiting to celebrate.

And you know how Warren liked parties.

It had taken them forty-five days of climbing over eighteen months.

675 pitons. 125 expansion bolts. 2,000 feet of rope. And a whole lot of blood and bruises.

But they'd done it.

El Cap would never be "unclimbable" again.

And best of all? He'd finally shown that Royal Robbins who was *really* king of the mountains.

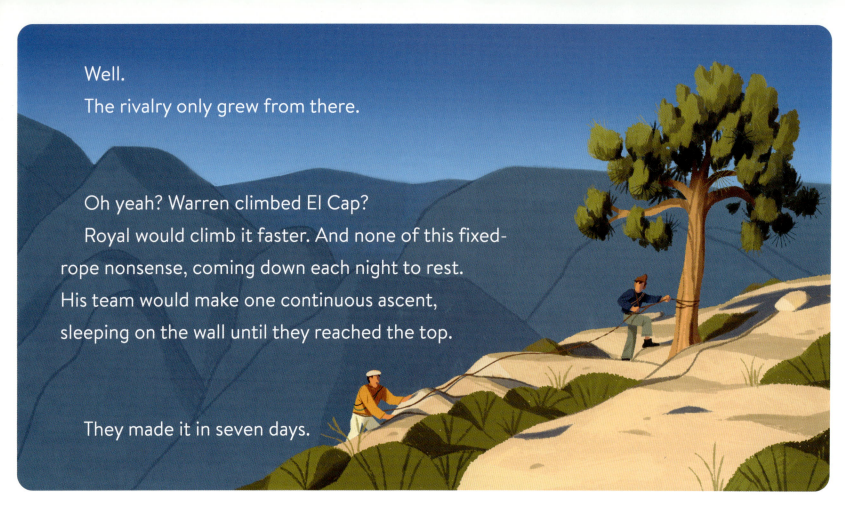

Well.
The rivalry only grew from there.

Oh yeah? Warren climbed El Cap?
Royal would climb it faster. And none of this fixed-rope nonsense, coming down each night to rest. His team would make one continuous ascent, sleeping on the wall until they reached the top.

They made it in seven days.

Fine. Warren would tackle another Yosemite challenge: an overhanging rock face called Leaning Tower. He climbed with partners and used fixed ropes.

So of course, Royal had to do that climb alone. With no fixed ropes. In the rain.

And just for good measure, he established a new route up El Cap.

All right, then. There were still plenty of unclimbed rocks in Yosemite. Warren would make a first ascent of the South Face of Mount Watkins.

And how about a new route up Half Dome, too?

But halfway up that climb, a huge storm swept in, trapping Warren and his partner on the wall. For two days and two nights, they shivered in soggy sleeping bags, huddled on the cliff in the icy wind. Finally, they gave up (you know how Warren hated that) and radioed for help. A helicopter arrived to drop a rescue team at the summit.

And who do you think came rappelling down in the dark to save them?

It just *had* to be Royal Robbins.

The rivalry wasn't just about *who* reached a summit first. It was also about *how* they got there.

Royal believed climbers ought to show the mountains some respect. He pushed for clean climbing, using minimal bolts, leaving behind as few traces of a climber's presence as possible.

Warren didn't care about that. He banged in however many bolts he needed to get up a wall. He just wanted to climb! Seriously. Who put Royal in charge of the mountains?

Warren wanted to climb something that would settle things once and for all. Something BIGGER and HARDER and MORE IMPRESSIVE. He'd noticed another amazing route up El Cap, along the Wall of Early Morning Light, or the Dawn Wall.

There was just one problem. All the great climbing features started 1,500 feet off the ground.

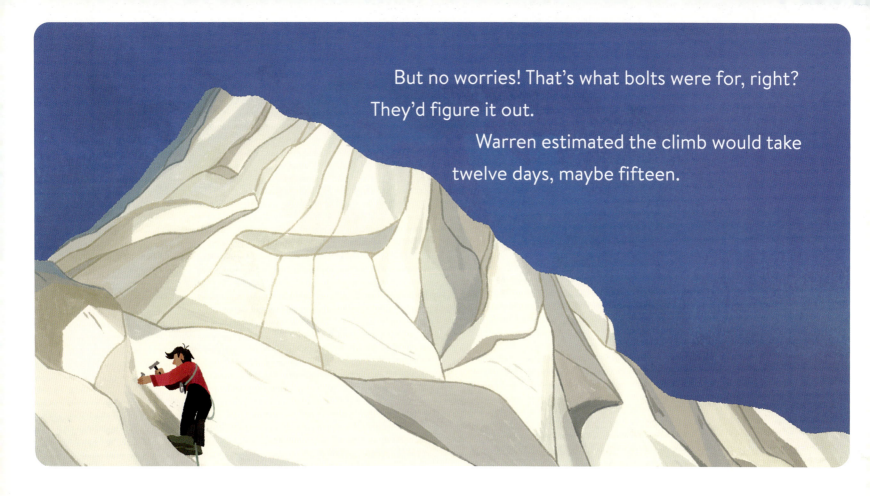

But no worries! That's what bolts were for, right? They'd figure it out.

Warren estimated the climb would take twelve days, maybe fifteen.

But the weather didn't cooperate.

The birds didn't cooperate, either.

Days passed. The climbers weren't making enough progress. When they reached a stretch with no cracks or holds, they hammered in bolts. Bolt after bolt after bolt, until they'd crossed a hundred feet of blank wall.

After two weeks on the wall, another storm blew in. They twisted and turned and shivered all night long. Their hammocks started to rip.

On the second day, a park ranger called up to offer them a rescue.

But you know how Warren felt about giving up. The climbers made it clear they did not want help.

A rescue is unwarranted, unwanted and will not be accepted.

Finally, the storm passed, and they started climbing again. They made some progress. But they also took some falls. And they were running out of food.

Warren turned down two more rescue attempts before they finally reached the summit.

By then, the leaves in the Valley had turned golden and started to fall.

Warren hoisted himself over the ledge and found a crowd waiting. Friends and reporters and photographers. There were photos and hugs, handshakes and backslaps. And food. SO. MUCH. FOOD.

And you know how Warren loved a party.

So what do you think Royal did when he heard about Warren's latest climb?

Two months later, Royal set out with a friend to make a *second* ascent of the Dawn Wall. Along with the usual gear, Royal brought a hammer and chisel. As he climbed, he began chopping off all those bolts that Warren had hammered into the rock.

Climb.

CHOP.

Climb.

CHOP.

Who did that Warren Harding think he was? If he couldn't climb a route without drilling in more than *three hundred* bolts, he had no business climbing it at all. Royal was going to erase the whole thing.

Climb.
CHOP.
Climb.
CHOP.

But that night on the wall, Royal couldn't sleep. Was he doing the right thing? This climb wasn't easy. What Warren had done—bolts or no bolts—was incredible. Like it or not, Royal was impressed.

He stopped chopping bolts, summitted in six days, and came down.

After that, Warren climbed some more rocks and Royal climbed some more rocks. But their rivalry sort of fizzled. Eventually, it grew into a quiet respect. Both men came to realize that maybe it had never been each other they were battling.

All those years, all those big walls, it was their own fear, their own limits they'd been fighting. They'd done it by climbing giant walls of granite in a place that made them feel more alive than anywhere else on Earth.

And did they conquer those mountains? Royal and Warren would tell you no. They knew the rocks had been around for millions of years before they ever showed up to climb them . . .

. . . and would be towering over Yosemite Valley long after they were gone.

AUTHOR'S NOTE

My son Jake introduced me to rock climbing and to Yosemite National Park, one of his favorite places on Earth. It was easy to see why, and I found myself wondering about the people who have tried climbing those massive cliffs. Our conversation led to Royal and Warren, sparking months of research and, eventually, this book.

I'd like to thank everyone who helped with research and fact-checking, especially Hannah Fleetwood, Jerry Gallwas, Liz Robbins, Jim Thomsen, Ken Yager, and everyone at the Yosemite Climbing Association for their work in preserving the history of Yosemite climbing.

Royal and Warren are gone now, but they left their mark on the sport of rock climbing. Royal's ethics led to a new style of climbing that had less of an impact on the environment and helped usher in the Leave No Trace guidelines that are a cornerstone of conservation today. Just like Royal and Warren, today's climbers aspire to their own first ascents, pushing the sport to even higher levels.

ROCK CLIMBING Q&A

When rock climbers spend days (or even weeks!) up on a wall, what do they eat and drink?

Rock climbers need to carry everything they'll eat and drink while they're on a big wall. That includes a gallon of water per day for each climber and high-energy foods that won't spoil. Meat jerky, fruit, bagels, nut butters, and trail mix are favorites!

Okay. But how do they go to the bathroom?

Depends. Are you asking about #1 or #2? Climbers often pee in empty water bottles and then dump them at the end of the climb. Pooping on a big wall is trickier. There are no bathrooms, so climbers don't have much privacy. When nature calls, they squat and relieve themselves into a plastic bag (often called a wag bag), which they seal and carry with them until they're off the wall and it can be thrown away.

Where do they sleep?

Climbers sleep on ledges when they're available. When they're not, climbers use a portaledge, a collapsible platform that hangs down from anchors placed in the wall.

Is rock climbing a dangerous sport?

You might see rock climbers scaling cliffs and imagine it's a lot more dangerous than other sports. However, the rate of injury for rock climbing is actually lower than it is for cycling, hockey, football, and soccer. When safety equipment such as ropes and harnesses are used properly, they go a long way in keeping climbers safe. Still, accidents happen, and on big walls they can be fatal. Yosemite National Park sees an average of 2.5 deaths per year out of the tens of thousands who rock climb there.

Did Royal Robbins and Warren Harding die in climbing accidents?

No. Rock climbing didn't kill Warren Harding; alcohol did. Warren loved the music and crowd of a party, but he also struggled with addiction and wasn't able to stop drinking, even when his health suffered. He died of liver failure at age seventy-seven. Royal Robbins died of an incurable brain disease when he was eighty-two.

OTHER ROCK STARS OF YOSEMITE NATIONAL PARK AND BEYOND

ROYAL ROBBINS and WARREN HARDING climbed with partners who were rock stars in their own right. Here's a closer look at those partners and others who have left their mark on the sport.

GEORGE ANDERSON made the first ascent of Half Dome in 1875. He went barefoot and drilled iron spikes into the rock for protection.

KAREEMAH BATTS began climbing in 2011 after losing part of her leg to cancer. She founded the Adaptive Climbing Group to support other climbers with disabilities.

JIM BRIDWELL made over a hundred first ascents in Yosemite, including the first one-day ascent of the Nose on El Capitan in 1975, with John Long and Billy Westbay.

TOMMY CALDWELL and KEVIN JORGESON made the first free ascent of El Capitan's Dawn Wall in 2015. That means they didn't use ladders or other aids for upward momentum as they climbed.

YVON CHOUINARD joined Royal Robbins, Chuck Pratt, and Tom Frost for the first ascent of the North America Wall on El Capitan in 1964.

MIKE CORBETT started climbing big walls in 1976 and summited El Capitan more than fifty times, earning the nickname Mr. El Cap.

GLEN DENNY joined Warren Harding and Al MacDonald for the first ascent of the West Face of Leaning Tower in 1961. His other first ascents include Astroman on Washington Column in 1959 and Dihedral Wall on El Capitan in 1962.

SASHA DIGIULIAN is a three-time US National Champion in rock climbing. She and her partner Jon Cardwell made the first free ascent of the Misty Wall next to Upper Yosemite Fall in 2017.

HANS FLORINE set a record for the most climbs up El Capitan, with over 180 ascents, and in 2012 achieved a speed record for the Nose with Alex Honnold (2 hours, 23 minutes, 46 seconds).

TOM FROST joined Royal Robbins and Chuck Pratt for the first ascent of the Salathé Wall on El Capitan in 1961. In 1964, he teamed up with Robbins, Pratt, and Yvon Chouinard to make the first ascent of the North America Wall.

JERRY GALLWAS joined Royal Robbins and Mike Sherrick for the first ascent of the Northwest Face of Half Dome in 1957.

CHELSEA GRIFFIE became the first Black woman to summit El Capitan when she and her partners climbed Lurking Fear in 2001.

LYNN HILL, one of the early successful women in the sport of rock climbing, made the first free ascent of the Nose on El Capitan in 1993.

ALEX HONNOLD is known for free solo ascents, a dangerous style of climbing without ropes or other safety gear. In 2017, he became the first person to free solo El Capitan.

RON KAUK lived at Yosemite's famous Camp 4 for decades. He made the first free ascent of the Astroman route on Washington Column in 1975 (with John Long and John Bachar) and the first ascent of the famous boulder problem Midnight Lightning in 1978.

LONNIE KAUK is a descendant of Chief Tenaya of the Ahwahneechee people in Yosemite. Born and raised in the Valley, Lonnie followed in his father Ron's footsteps and loves climbing. Lonnie made the second ascent of the boulder Too Big to Flail in 2013.

DON LAURIA partnered with Royal Robbins for the second ascent of the Dawn Wall in 1971.

BETHANY LEBEWITZ noticed that not many people on the crag looked like her, so in 2016 she launched Brown Girls Climb, a community aimed at making the sport of rock climbing more inclusive.

KAI LIGHTNER holds ten Youth National Championship titles and is a five-time Youth World Championship medalist. In 2020, he launched the nonprofit Climbing for Change to open the sport to more people of color.

WAYNE MERRY made several first ascents in Yosemite Valley and made history when he summited El Capitan with Warren Harding and George Whitmore in 1958.

ADAM ONDRA has won multiple World Championship titles in lead climbing and bouldering. In 2016, he completed the second free ascent of the Dawn Wall, and in only in eight days, less than half the time of the first ascent.

DEAN POTTER made the first free solo ascent of Heaven at Glacier Point in 2006. He held the record for the fastest ascent of the Nose until it was broken by Honnold and Florine.

CHUCK PRATT made a number of first ascents in Yosemite, including the North Face of Fairview Dome in Tuolumne Meadows with Wally Reed in 1958 and Astroman on Washington Column in Yosemite Valley with Warren Harding and Glen Denny in 1959.

LIZ ROBBINS became the first woman to summit a Yosemite big wall when she and Royal Robbins climbed the Regular Northwest Face of Half Dome together in 1967.

BETH RODDEN made the first ascent of Meltdown, next to Yosemite's Upper Cascade Falls, in 2008. She partnered with Tommy Caldwell for the first free ascent of Lurking Fear and the second free ascent of the Nose.

GALEN ROWELL made dozens of first ascents in Yosemite, including the South Face of Half Dome with Warren Harding in 1970. Later, at age fifty-seven, he became the oldest person to climb El Capitan in a single day.

JOHN SALATHÉ made the first ground-up ascent of Yosemite's Lost Arrow Spire in 1947. He was a blacksmith whose climbing experiences led him to invent the modern piton.

ASHIMA SHIRAISHI is a World Champion climber with multiple first-female and youngest ascents. In 2012, at age ten, she became the youngest person to climb a V13 boulder problem (Crown of Aragorn, in Hueco Tanks, Texas).

GEORGE WHITMORE was part of Warren Harding's team that summited the Nose in 1958. Whitmore was also a conservationist who helped create the Kaiser Wilderness southeast of Yosemite and fought for the California Wilderness Act of 1984.

DON WILSON joined Royal Robbins, Jerry Gallwas, and Warren Harding for an attempt on the Northwest Face of Half Dome in 1955 but failed to summit. He went on to successfully make several other first ascents in Yosemite.

ROCK CLIMBING AND YOSEMITE NATIONAL PARK RESOURCES

BOOKS

How to Solve a Problem: The Rise (and Falls) of a Rock-Climbing Champion, by Ashima Shiraishi, illustrated by Yao Xiao (Make Me a World, 2020).

Rock Stars!: True Stories of Extreme Climbing Adventures, by Steve Bramucci (National Geographic Kids, 2018).

WEBSITES

The National Park Service's "Climbing" page has information about types of climbing, safety, and the history of the sport. nps.gov/subjects/climbing/index.htm

Yosemite Climbing Association works to raise awareness of Yosemite climbing and preserve the history of the sport. yosemiteclimbing.org

If you're visiting Yosemite and want to try rock climbing, Yosemite Mountaineering School and Guide Service offers classes and outings. yosemite.com/things-to-do/adventure-activities/yosemite-mountaineering-school-guide-service

Or, if you're more of a curious observer, the Ask a Climber station near El Capitan Meadow has you covered. yosemite.org/projects/ask-a-climber-program

SELECTED SOURCES

Ament, Pat. *Royal Robbins: Spirit of the Age*. Stackpole Books, 1998.

Harding, Warren, and Beryl Knauth. *Downward Bound: A Mad! Guide to Rock Climbing*. Joseph Reidhead & Company, 2016.

Robbins, Royal. *My Life*. 3 vols. Royal Robbins Adventures, 2009–2012.

Roper, Steve. *Camp 4: Recollections of a Yosemite Rockclimber*. Mountaineers Books, 1994.

Scott, Doug. *Big Wall Climbing: Development, Techniques, and Aids*. Oxford University Press, 1974.

Taylor, Joseph E., III. *Pilgrims of the Vertical: Yosemite Rock Climbers and Nature at Risk*. Harvard University Press, 2010.

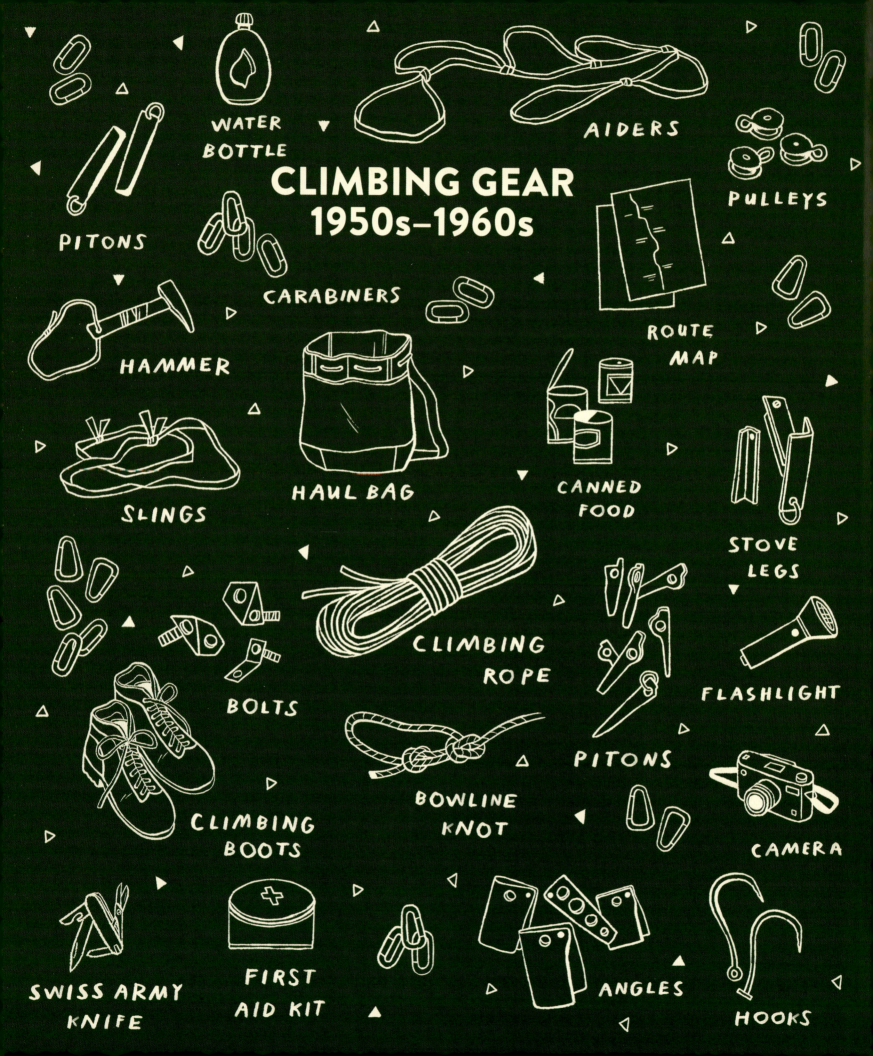